Unreality Check:
The Mindful Way to Heal Depersonalization and Derealization

Written by a former sufferer

Ravelle Arianne

Revised. Originally Published April 2021
ISBN 978-1-7775888-0-9

inherentpeace.com

DEDICATION

To those who have wondered if they're living inside a TV.

Disclaimer

This work is intended for informational purposes only.

Information provided in this book may be triggering for those suffering from mental illness.

This book provides general information, and it is not intended to diagnose, prescribe, treat, or cure any disease or illness.

Nothing contained herein is intended to constitute medical advice or medical care and treatment.

Do not delay, disregard, or discontinue professional medical advice or stop medical treatments without speaking to a healthcare professional.

Results are not guaranteed.

The ideas discussed in this book are based on the personal opinions and experiences of the author.

The author is not a medical professional, nor claims to be one.

The author cannot be held liable for any losses or damages you incur either directly or indirectly related to this book.

Acknowledgements

Bhante Saranapala, for teaching me about Buddhism and the heart of mindfulness, and to face my pain with self-compassion, and for helping me return to meditation.

Ursula Doran, for helping me understand that thoughts are not facts and the difference between thoughts and emotions.

My husband, for your love, endless support, and patience, and for always being my Editor in Chief.

My family, for always believing in my recovery and encouraging me to share my story.

Kimberley Marquis, for inspiring me to dream, for your support, guidance, and friendship.

Chaz, Bella, and Odin, for being the greatest furriest friends ever and for always brightening my day, just by being.

The Buddha, Mooji, Ajahn Chah, Eckhart Tolle, Ramana Maharshi, Nisargadatta Maharaj, Jalāl ad-Dīn Mohammad Rūmī, Thích Nhất Hạnh, and Michael A. Singer for inspiring me to believe in and eventually recognize my inherent peace and freedom.

A Course in Miracles, for being a beautiful reminder that fear only exists in illusions.

Bhagavad Gita, Upanishads, and Avadhuta Gita, for the ancient teachings of India that have awoken my mind to the timeless Self.

The Inherent Peace Community, thank you for your continued support, trust, and feedback, and for inspiring and encouraging me to share my writing.

Table of Contents

Introduction

Based on my lived experience, healing depersonalization and derealization (DPDR) is possible. After suffering for most of my life, I have fully recovered from DPDR using mindfulness, mindfulness-based cognitive therapy (MBCT), and spiritual practices and teachings. Although some mental health professionals still believe that there is no cure for DPDR, I hope to change some minds by sharing my experience of healing with mindfulness.

I also want to be clear that I am not a mental health expert, and I don't have the wisdom of a monk or sage. I am simply sharing what I've experienced and learned for myself. While creating this self-help guide and workbook, I discovered countless people who have also recovered from their symptoms. You will find their stories online and in other self-published books. I encourage you to look for them and find hope in them.

We all have different experiences, and DPDR is not the same for everyone. So, I am here to add my story as a former sufferer, and share the methods, teachings, and ideas that I found beneficial.

If you have been experiencing DPDR, it may feel like you are alone in the way you experience life. Additionally, your mind may be full of doubts and fears. Regardless of where you are now, try to have an open mind and let go of all your expectations as you read. The more open you are, the more you will get out of this book.

For some, the ideas discussed may seem abstract due to the tendency to identify with the mind. Nonetheless, the practices are intended to help you realize the true purpose of the theory. So, it is more important to utilize the exercises instead of fixating on the text.

On the surface, the worksheets and practices may seem simple to some, but healing requires work and openness. I hope you will give them all a fair chance and take your time going through them because they were the medicine that made my recovery possible. So, I encourage you to do your best to use the exercises regularly.

May this book comfort you on your way to freedom, and may everything provided here make your healing inevitable, as it was for me.

Preface

I'm not sure where it all started but I suspect trauma had a role to play. When I was a baby, I almost choked to death, and although I don't consciously remember the experience, I am certain that my subconscious does.

Also, I grew up in Trinidad and Tobago, and when I was around 5 years old, I remember almost drowning at the beach. A wave knocked me over and I was submerged into the water as the ocean current began to pull me. I couldn't tell which way was up or down, but suddenly my dad pulled me to safety.

So, some of my first memories are related to trauma and DPDR, and I recall having symptoms even as a child. In fact, for most of my life, I felt empty. I struggled to connect with the world and the people around me. Likewise, I frequently questioned my reality.

When I was about six years old, I remember looking at my mother and wondering if we were inside a TV. I looked at her, and she didn't seem real to me. It was frightening.

As I got older, my language developed, and a line of questioning began:
"Are other people real? Do they have feelings? Am I real? Why am I here?"

Feeling Disconnected, "Not Normal"

This existential thinking continued, and I felt like I was in a dream. Likewise, the world around me seemed distorted and I felt dead inside. Moreover, I felt devoid of emotion, aside from anxiety and the occasional bursts of anger.

During my high school years, I began to self-harm hoping to feel something. Instead, I continued to feel detached from the world, my body, thoughts, and emotions. Furthermore, my loved ones seemed like strangers and when I looked in the mirror, I felt estranged and detached from my own image.

One day, I tried to explain the experience to my mother, and I told her I felt like I had no soul, as if I was not here at all. Eventually, I realized that my experience was "not normal". Or rather, at the time I didn't understand what it was or how common it is.

Healing from Depersonalization and Derealization

For a long time, my experience with DPDR was not addressed by my mental health support team. So, I never knew what to make of it, and I did not know if it would ever go away.

Moreover, I had not considered the possibility of healing because I didn't understand DPDR. Until one day, I began to write down and analyze my thoughts and emotions.

By mere coincidence, I gained tremendous insight from that period of writing and introspection. I began to understand my experience on a deeper level, with mindful awareness and acceptance.

Consequently, once I addressed the psychological causes that engendered DPDR, the effect I experienced was complete healing. Yes, *complete healing*.

Now, I know what it's like when you're in a dark place and someone tells you, "you're going to be okay, you can get through this." That used to bother me because I felt invalidated. And I know how isolating, terrifying, and weird DPDR can be. But then again, "Healing Depersonalization and Derealization" is in the title of this book. So, for right now, it's enough if you can just keep an open mind.

There were so many nights I wanted to end my life, and so many days that I just didn't see the point in living. I also had other mental health issues, and I knew I wanted to heal, but I didn't know how or if it was even possible.

So, have courage, because you are more resilient and powerful than you know. Trust that as you read this book, your awareness will increase, and have hope that you will grow in understanding and eventually break free of DPDR for good.

Escape the False Belief that Healing is not Possible

When I started blogging about mindfulness and mental health, a young man who suffered from DPDR reached out to me. He was told by his mental healthcare providers that there is no cure for DPDR.

A belief that he and many hold strongly because it is what they have been told. Yet, ask yourself: **what is the cost of not having hope? How do you feel without it?**

The news that healing is not possible causes undue fear and suffering—which is the opposite of what you need when seeking support.

I was lucky enough to have escaped this perception from my healthcare providers, mainly because we rarely discussed the issue. And at the time I thought, *who am I to go against what his healthcare providers have told him?*

Of course, acceptance is vital to finding peace and happiness, but no one can predict all the possibilities that the future holds.

With that said, my conversations with this gentleman motivated me to create this self-help guide and workbook. So, I hope to reach all those who remain open to the possibility of healing.

In fact, from my experience, healing is a reality, and reality is greater than hope.

Worksheets to help you build self-awareness, heal, and cultivate mindfulness are provided throughout this book. Note, these worksheets can also be helpful to manage anxiety, stress, depression, and panic attacks.

Section 1: Background

What is Depersonalization, Derealization, and Dissociation?

Symptoms

What It Feels Like

The Root Cause

Demystifying Depersonalization and Derealization

Cultivating Love and Compassion for Yourself

The Positive Intention

A Letter to DPDR

What is Depersonalization, Derealization, and Dissociation?

Here is a basic and brief look at the definitions, differences, and symptoms of depersonalization, derealization, and dissociation.

Definitions

- **Depersonalization**:

A sense of detachment from oneself and identity, including detachment from one's body and mind, as though one is an outside observer of one's experience rather than a participant.

- **Derealization:**

Classified by a sense of unreality—when things or people seem unreal.

- **Dissociation**:

A broader scope of detachment ranging from the sense of detachment from immediate surroundings to a severe sense of detachment from physical, emotional, and mental experience.

Note:

The difference is that depersonalization relates to how you perceive yourself, while derealization relates to how you perceive your surroundings and other people. The healing process is the same for both. Dissociation is a general sense of detachment, and it is more common.

References:
American Psychiatric Association. (2013). Diagnostic and statistical manual of mental disorders (5th ed.). https://doi.org/10.1176/appi.books.9780890425596.
Heydrich L, et al. Depersonalization- and derealization-like phenomena of epileptic origin. Ann Clin Transl Neurol. 2019 Sep;6(9):1739-1747. doi: 10.1002/acn3.50870. Epub 2019 Aug 22.

Symptoms

You may already be familiar with some, if not all the symptoms, but let's take an objective look to build further awareness and understanding.

Depersonalization Symptoms

-   Feeling empty, or detached from your body, thoughts, and feelings.
-   The sense that your body, legs, or arms appear distorted, enlarged, or shrunken, or that your head is wrapped in cotton.
-   Feeling like you're not in control of your speech or movements.
-   Emotional or physical numbness of your senses.
-   A sense that your memories lack emotion, and that they may not be your own.

Derealization Symptoms

-   Feelings of being alienated from your surroundings.
-   Surroundings and objects appear distorted, blurry, colorless, two-dimensional, or artificial, or a heightened awareness of your surroundings.
-   Feeling like you're living in a movie or a dream, or that you are behind a glass wall.
-   Distortions in the perception of time (ie. recent events feeling like distant past).
-   Feeling emotionally disconnected from others, including loved ones.
-   Unable to recognize yourself in the mirror.

References:
American Psychiatric Association. (2013). Diagnostic and statistical manual of mental disorders (5th ed.).
https://doi.org/10.1176/appi.books.9780890425596.
David Spiegel. "Depersonalization/Derealization Disorder." (2019). https://www.merckmanuals.com/professional/psychiatric-disorders/dissociative-disorders/depersonalization-derealization-disorder.

What It Feels Like

In high school, I experienced more numbness, apathy, zoning out, I didn't really know what was going on and everything felt *blah*. Nothing moved me, not even funerals. I wanted so badly to cry with everyone and to care about things. I felt heartless and soulless. That's one of the reasons I started to self-harm. Pain and sadness were welcomed feelings for me, because feeling disconnected was lifeless.

When I was 21, I started to feel more. It was as if all my emotions that I had bottled up over the last 21 years came to the surface. I exploded with intense feelings, and the DPDR kept arising and passing. I went through alternating states; DPDR, emotional burst, DPDR, eruption of anger, and sometimes everything at once. It was only then I started to miss the consistency of DPDR.

Different people experience DPDR differently because we all have unique life experiences. One person told me he felt like his head was wrapped in cotton and he kept losing time. Someone else told me they feel like a ghost and it's like they leave their body.

A lot of us describe a dreamlike quality to our experience and feeling robotic. That's why I enjoyed the movie Inception and the TV show Westworld. They depict living in a dreamworld or simulation. I felt like they validated my experience. Though, another friend with DPDR found Westworld triggering and couldn't watch it.

One lady shared her DPDR experience and described it as feeling separated from what was going on around her, as if she was not an active participant in her own life. Another woman talked about her difficulties with recognizing her friends and wondering if they are real.

You may have experienced all the above or have a different perspective entirely. My point is, we all have unique experiences with DPDR. Whatever *your* experience is, it is valid even if others don't understand or agree with it.

The Root Cause

So Why Exactly Do You Experience DPDR?

It is not fully known what causes DPDR. However, it has been linked to trauma, sleep deprivation, anxiety, significant loss, drugs, and intense stress. In the case of one man, he improved his DPDR symptoms by addressing his low testosterone levels. So, it may be worth checking with your healthcare providers to see whether physiological factors are potentially impacting you.

With that said, the consensus is to begin minimizing your stress and removing triggers, *because anxiety and stress feed DPDR.*

Depersonalization and Derealization are Fear-Based Responses

It seems dissociation is a *coping mechanism* allowing you a psychological retreat from negative feelings and experiences. It is said to be a *defense mechanism* like the *fight* or *flight* response. Dissociation and DPDR are associated with our *freeze* response. Fight, flight, and freeze are all fear-based responses.

If you have ever approached a rabbit, sometimes it runs off but other times it doesn't move. Apparently, the rabbit thinks that you cannot see it when it freezes. In humans, it would be like giving a presentation and blanking out because you can't remember your points and your nerves take over.

Another way to look at the freeze response is if you were about to drown, panicking would not serve you. Instead, detaching from your experience would give you a chance to remain calm and determine a course of action.

With DPDR you no longer experience life fully through your body, emotions, and sense perceptions because your attention withdraws from these experiences. Instead, you begin to experience life primarily through *thought*. **Your mind becomes the foreground of your life, while physical reality becomes the background.**

During traumatic events this is helpful rather than harmful. DPDR helps you cope with overwhelming feelings, but it does so through avoidance. Consequently, your psyche will "detach" from your experience, but this is not a physical detachment.

For this reason, *fear* is the root cause of DPDR, and *thought* engenders the perception of unreality. So, both need to be addressed.

Demystifying Depersonalization and Derealization

DPDR is common in about 1-2% of the general population[1]. However, many people have had at least one episode in their life. Furthermore, it is not uncommon for people to experience dissociation when they are hung-over, tired, overwhelmed, or afraid. For some, dissociating is a desirable part of smoking marijuana. Additionally, most people experience dissociation at some point in their lives.

For instance, the loss of a loved one can be so painful that it can cause someone to unconsciously withdraw their attention from their emotional and physical experience.

As a result, they don't connect and *feel* their pain. This helps them cope and eventually they will reconnect with their surroundings, mind, and body when their experience is less intense and painful.

However, when it comes to DPDR, this detachment becomes an uncomfortable and intense pattern, likely due to past trauma and habitual dissociation.

In summary, we start off in a neutral state, until there is a trigger. When we can't handle the emotions, we dissociate, and following dissociation is DPDR. So, to heal, we'll have to back track until we reach our original neutral starting point.

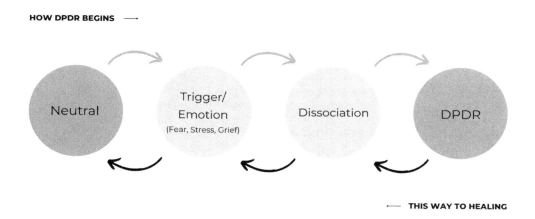

Once the DPDR symptoms are addressed, we will need to reconnect, and then move through our emotions to return to our original state, which is calm and peaceful.

Reference:
1. Hunter, EC et al. The epidemiology of depersonalisation and derealisation. A systematic review. Social Psychiatry and Psychiatric Epidemiology. January 2004. 39 (1): 9–18. doi:10.1007/s00127-004-0701-4.

Cultivating Love and Compassion For Yourself

Sometimes DPDR distorts your perception of time, which is also common during a panic attack or when you're under extreme stress. Hours feel like minutes and weeks feel like days. This experience is like living in a dream. Have you ever nodded off and dreamt an entire world, only to wake up in amazement that just a few minutes had passed?

For years, DPDR seemed constant. Once I began to heal, I saw how DPDR progressed and persisted. As I started to recover, I continued to dissociate and experience panic attacks for some time.

I remember one day my anxiety levels reached a breaking point. My heart was fearfully racing, and I began crying uncontrollably. Crippled by desperation and fear, I retreated to hide in my closet, where my husband tried to console me.

Everything felt like a blur. It became difficult to recognize my husband because I was so far gone. I had to keep reminding myself it was him and that I was safe. Lost in the experience of inner pain, everything felt unreal.

When I finally stopped crying, my husband held me, and I began to connect back to my body. Practicing mindful awareness, I did not want to reject my pain because I was already on my healing journey. At this point, I knew **the only way through pain was to allow it to move freely through me.**

The next day, I found out that I was crying and thrashing around for 2 hours, but to me, it felt like 10 minutes.

In this case, I was **triggered** by work stress, and I felt anxious for several days. Next, the **anxiety intensified**, and I started to **dissociate**. Once I was in the thick of it, **DPDR** kicked in, and my experience felt unreal.

This is how DPDR tries to protect you, its positive intention is to shield you from pain and discomfort. So much of your energy is pulled into psychological suffering that you mentally detach, making it difficult to be aware of most things, including time.

Sometimes we judge ourselves harshly when we are suffering because we believe that we should or shouldn't be a certain way. *Non-judging* is part of practicing mindfulness, but this doesn't mean that we never make any judgments.

Rather, we recognize that it is the nature of the mind to judge ourselves, others, and our experiences. Letting go of judgment means cultivating kindness and compassion.

For this reason, when I became triggered, my task was not to beat myself up. Nor was it to invalidate my emotions. My role was not to get angry or condemn myself when I realized the gaps in time. My only duty was to love myself and show myself the same compassion that my husband showed me.

If you are concerned by the gaps in time you experience, do your best to reassure yourself that this is a common experience for anyone who has had trauma in their lives or who is under a lot of emotional stress. And although *everyone* feels out of control and lost at times, you have a perspective that no one else has.

So, just be compassionate with yourself because you are dealing with a lot. Don't beat yourself up, don't invalidate your feelings, and try not to condemn yourself for experiencing DPDR. Otherwise, you may create more pain for yourself.

If life is slowing down or speeding up, make taking care of yourself your primary goal. You deserve love and kindness. Whatever has happened to you, and whatever is to come, **be there for yourself through it all, like a great friend.**

"A true friend is one who stands by you in need."

— The Buddha, Sigālovāda Sutta

If you go to war with yourself and your experience, you will not know peace and every day will be a fight and a struggle.

The Positive Intention

Although depersonalization and derealization are uncomfortable and at times terrifying, thankfully they are not inherently dangerous.

Bear in mind, the positive intention behind this form of detachment manifests to shield you from painful experiences.

When I was a child, I had a lot of anxiety and often felt lost and alone. Likewise, in high school, I experienced more trauma.

So, DPDR was a welcome relief, safeguarding me from intense suffering.

At some point, it is likely that DPDR stepped in to help you navigate life.

As a result, when you look at depersonalization and derealization through the eyes of compassion, you see that its sole aim is to help you cope.

This shift in perspective helps you to approach your experience with compassion and patience, rather than tension and fear.

In fact, making peace with your experience through the recognition of its positive intention helps dissolve this pattern altogether.

While DPDR is no longer helpful, try to recognize that it has served you in the past.

Making Peace

While this may seem like an unusual thing to do, just imagine for a moment, you are speaking to your DPDR, as if it were a person.

This exercise will help you gain space, express your grievances, and make peace with DPDR so you can move forward.

Notice how you feel about DPDR but recall its positive intention. Thank it for being there when you needed it. Then, take a deep breath and let your DPDR know that it is no longer necessary, and you are ready to let it go.

The more you relax about the presence of your DPDR, the less you intensify it. So, for the moment, allow it space to be a part of your experience while we work through the healing process.

Make peace with it, knowing that it came when you needed it, and trust that it will dissolve once you've learned new ways of coping, thinking, and being.

A Letter to DP/DR

ACKNOWLEDGE, REFLECT, ACCEPT, AND RELEASE

MINDFULNESS SKILLS:

- Face your pain with openness, compassion, and let go of judgment
- Accept and allow space for your experience to be what it is in this moment

Acknowledge the suffering depersonalization and derealization has caused you. Write as if you are speaking to your DP/DR, tell it how it has affected you, and openly express any pain it has caused you throughout your life.

Reflect on your DP/DR's positive intention and write to it, letting it know you understand the reason it came into your life. If you feel up to it, you can even thank it for being there when you needed it.

Create a short message to yourself for the next time you experience your symptoms to help you make peace with how you are feeling. For example: *I am experiencing DP/DR, and I am going to be okay, it is not here to hurt me, I will allow space for my healing.*

Write to your DP/DR to let it know that it is no longer useful and that you are ready to experience life without it. Let it know what it would mean to you to be free of it.

Section 2: Principles

What Exactly is Mindfulness?

Before mindfulness gained popularity in the west, its origins began thousands of years ago in Hindu meditation practices, before the Buddha was born, and it eventually branched out into Buddhism. So, we can thank India, the Buddha, and the east for these teachings and scriptures that are helping many people find peace in their lives.

In fact, Buddhist teachings have influenced modern psychotherapy. Mindfulness-Based Cognitive Therapy (MBCT) utilizes the ancient principles of mindfulness because it brings balance, clarity, insight, peace, and equanimity to the mind.

The spirit of mindfulness is to consciously bring your attention to your present experience without resistance, judgment, interpretation, or expectation. When we are mindful, we encounter life without the influence of our perceptions. This makes our experiences serene and tranquil, calming our fears and quieting our minds.

Some mindful practices focus your attention on a specific object (i.e., the breath), while others relate to being aware of the present moment. The former focuses the mind more deeply, but the latter is easier to do. Nevertheless, both are beneficial. And I encourage you to try all the practices in this book to reap the full benefits.

How does mindfulness heal DPDR?

Practicing mindfulness helps you uncover and break the negative cycles that cause DPDR. **Without mindfulness, unconscious patterns continue to run your life ruling your behavior, perceptions, and mood.**

Mindfulness connects us to everything that is currently dissociated from our awareness and corrects distortions in our perception of reality due to our thoughts. With mindful awareness, you can break the shackles of unreality and DPDR.

3 Truths of Mindfulness

The Buddha spoke of *3 marks of existence* that seem to be intuitively understood by DPDR sufferers. With a little added wisdom from Buddhist teachings, these 3 points can help you let go of DPDR patterns.

1st: Annicā – Impermanence

Everything by nature is constantly changing: the seasons, our planet, and even our bodies. Nothing lasts forever.

With the realization of impermanence, we see that there isn't anything we can cling to. As a result, "non-attachment" is an aspect of mindfulness, but it is not the same as the "detachment" experienced with DPDR.

Non-attachment means we can hold things and engage in the world, without clinging too tightly, understanding that they do not last.

As you face your DPDR patterns, remember that these patterns are also subject to change. Thoughts, states, and emotions come and go, they are not worth holding on to because they are fleeting.

In the end, impermanence teaches us that trying to hold on to any aspect of our experience will result in pain. However, learning to let go frees us from our expectations, desires, and worries.

2nd: Dukkha – Suffering

The mind by nature is restless, focuses on the negative, resists the way things are, and is full of desire.

Challenges are inevitable in life and resisting them creates a constant sense of lack. So, when obstacles arise you can either accept them or make them into an enemy. Acceptance allows you to deal with situations with ease and grace as opposed to creating more pain.

DPDR thinking also follows the pattern of resisting unpleasantness and focusing on negativity. For this reason, making peace with your experience eases your suffering.

With mindful awareness, you will begin to recognize when your mind is leading you toward unhappiness, so you are not swept away by it.

3rd: Anattā - Not-Self

DPDR sufferers often struggle with their sense of identity, questioning who they are. Yet, one identity often remains: the identity with DPDR and perceiving oneself as *a person with DPDR.*

This leads to a dark place. You are not any of your experiences, and it's best not to cling to them. Emotional, mental, and physical phenomena are all transient. They come and go; we are simply aware of them.

There is no sense in clinging to anything as part of your identity because everything changes. Additionally, being lost in the mental philosophy of "who you are" is not conducive to your freedom from DPDR.

Yes, DPDR creates challenges, obstacles, and pain, but believing that this is *who you are*, only creates further suffering.

No one's illness defines them; DPDR does not define you. It may walk with you every day of your life, like a shadow that follows you around, but *you* are not that shadow.

Letting go of your identification with DPDR may feel like you are losing a part of yourself. This can be uncomfortable, but this identity is built upon suffering. And *experiencing* your symptoms is not the same as *identifying* with them.

The practice is to let go of the attachment to a self-concept. You experience DPDR, but it isn't you.

Reflection

- On a scale of 1-10, how much has DPDR become a part of your identity? _____
- How has DPDR impacted the ideas you have about yourself? (i.e., does it make you think of yourself as broken? special? abnormal? lost? an over thinker? etc.)

_____

_____

- Do you truly believe that healing is possible? (yes/no)
- Can you let go of your judgments, beliefs, and preconceived notions about DPDR and about healing? (yes/no)
- What is one thing you are willing to try to make healing possible? (i.e., practice mindfulness, keep an open mind, practice self-compassion, have hope, etc.)

_____

_____

Uncovering Patterns

Becoming Aware of Unhealthy Patterns

Breaking it All Down

To illustrate how DPDR becomes a pattern, you'll need to understand the 3 components of your experience:

More importantly, you'll need to understand their differences and how they affect each other. For example, many of us say things like "I feel…" to express a thought. For instance, "I feel worthless." Worthless is not a feeling, it is a thought. It is a *concept* you have about yourself, rather than an *emotion*.

This is an important distinction since our thoughts feed our emotions.

Furthermore, feelings and physical sensations are the measures we use to validate our reality, but the thoughts influencing them are often unconscious.

So, now it will be up to you to become aware of these thoughts, and mindfulness can help you do this.

Recognizing Links

Your Mood and Physical Responses are Linked to Your Thoughts

Humans don't *only* cry when they are sad, but when they're happy too.

Likewise, the physical sensations linked to excitement are the same as the physical responses of nervousness (i.e. heart beating rapidly), but whether you are excited or nervous is determined by your thinking.

Imagine you are about to give a presentation to a large audience. On the one hand, if you are thinking '*people are going to think I'm weird, I know I'm going to mess up...*'

You will be nervous.

Whereas, if you are thinking '*people are going to love my presentation, this is going to blow their minds, I can't wait to share my findings, this is my best work yet!*'

Then, you will probably be excited.

In both scenarios, you will experience an increased heart rate. The same physical sensations will take place in the body, but your emotions will be determined by your thoughts.

For this reason, the *mental* experience of DPDR pervades your physical and emotional experience.

This may be obvious to some, but we don't always realize it in the heat of the moment. With mindful awareness, we can practice seeing this dynamic and letting go of our unhelpful thoughts. Alternatively, we can practice reframing and changing our thinking to find more balance.

"All that we are is the result of what we have thought: it is founded on our thoughts, it is made up of our thoughts. If a man speaks or acts with a pure thought, happiness follows him, like a shadow that never leaves him." — **Dhammapada**

The Role of the Mind:

How Your Mind Magnifies Depersonalization

The Role of your Mind's Attention

If you are watching a movie, your attention withdraws from your surroundings.

So, the room you are in is no longer experienced by you. The room hasn't disappeared, rather your attention has moved away from it.

It isn't until you shift your attention back to your surroundings that you can connect with the space you are in. In the same way your attention can be absorbed by a movie, it can also be absorbed in thought.

Those with DPDR *think* about their experience instead of being *aware* of it because their attention is normally immersed in their minds.

As a result, it is no surprise that when you dissociate, you have a harder time remembering things. No one remembers something their attention had not been on in the first place.

This can also appear to distort time. Really, the cause of memory problems and lapses in time amongst DPDR sufferers is due to a difficulty in focusing. This is common with stress, anxiety, and trauma, which affect your ability to concentrate.

So, healing depersonalization and derealization with mindfulness means paying attention to all aspects of your experience and learning to shift your focus from the mind to the present moment. This takes time, just as one trains the body to build muscle, mindfulness trains the mind to be relaxed and focused.

The Role of your Mind's Thought Patterns

Many people do not live in the present moment, and when you suffer from DPDR, the present moment is lost.

Right now, when you look around or experience yourself, you are looking through layers of conscious and unconscious thoughts.

Rather than looking with pure awareness, we are often seeing our own thoughts being reflected in the world. Thus, your perception becomes distorted.

These thoughts are frequently dissociated from your awareness too. So, it is going to take some time to catch them.

For instance, you may unconsciously be thinking *I am in a movie, I am in a dream, I am not real, everything seems fuzzy, I feel weird, this doesn't make sense, I don't get it*, etc.

Note that weird is not an emotion—it is impossible to *feel* weird. Although, it is totally possible to interpret or *think* of yourself as weird.

In truth, the previous statements, including *I feel weird* are only thoughts, not emotional or physical experiences. Whereas the emotion underneath the thoughts might be shame, fear, or sadness. And the physical sensations might be tension, shallow breathing, or rapid heart rate.

Imagine how you will feel once these thoughts are gone. The emotional and physical sensations associated with these thoughts will also lessen and dissolve in due course.

With mindfulness, you will be able to recognize these thought-patterns, build your awareness, focus your attention, and connect with the present moment. In time, the layers of mental depersonalization and derealization will be stripped away.

The Present Moment

Many people live life on autopilot, and those who are more susceptible to mental illness have an even harder time connecting to the present moment due to their suffering.

When a Buddhist monk first told me that I needed to "focus on the present moment", I had no idea what he was talking about. At the time, my mind was saying, *I'm right here, aren't I? What does he mean focus on the present moment?*

Truthfully, I thought I was already present, but I wasn't because I was just hearing my own thoughts. I was unable to see how my attention was consumed by my mind.

Focusing on the present moment without mental projections is the essence of mindfulness.

In fact, when you are not thinking, you probably aren't experiencing DPDR at all. For instance, some of the following questions may seem silly, but answer them honestly:

- Do you experience DPDR when you sleep?

- Were you born with it?

- Can you say for sure that you have *always* had DPDR? If not, what changed?

- Think back to a time when you were enjoying yourself, was DPDR part of your experience?

- When you are focused or absorbed in a task, do you experience DPDR?

- When do you notice DPDR most? Is it when you think about it?

- What thoughts do you have when you notice your DPDR?

- Does DPDR come and go?

Regardless of how you answered the above questions, you will find that as you build your awareness, your mind is constantly bombarding you with thoughts and negativity. Likewise, when your focus is on your DPDR, it seems to intensify.

The Mind's Resistance to the Present Moment

The mind loves to fixate on the past and worry about the future. It resists the present moment. So, to heal DPDR, you'll want to train your mind to be present. This may seem difficult at first since the nature of the mind is restless. Buddhists call it "the monkey mind" because it jumps from one thought to another. Be patient and gentle with yourself and notice how the mind drifts from past to future. This awareness is all that is needed for now.

The Past

When your mind is lost in the past, it may be replaying painful memories or perpetuating guilt, regret, anger, a sense of loss, or shame. This creates pain in the present moment and can fill you with a sense of dread.

For instance, if you are driving and someone cuts you off, it may fill you with anger. When you go home and tell your loved one about it, you may continue to feel angry. If you go to bed thinking about it, your anger will also go to bed with you.

The same happens when trauma is relived in the mind. You may already know the pain that comes from thoughts about the past. As you learn to focus more on the present moment, the past is released, and so is the pain it brings.

The Future

Alternatively, when your thoughts are drawn to the future, this can cause anxiety and fear.

The mind is often riddled with uncertainty because it cannot predict what will happen. Yet, it continues to imagine different scenarios and outcomes.

The mind's tendency towards worst-case scenarios may have been helpful long ago. For instance, if you heard a rustling in the bushes, it could have been a mouse or a lion, and assuming the worst would increase your chances of survival.

We've now evolved with this negativity bias.

However, in today's world, it just doesn't work. In fact, it causes more harm than good, leaving many people in a state of constant worry and stress.

Furthermore, merely *thinking* about the future isn't going to *change* or *solve* anything.

Really, the future only exists in your mind because you are creating stories about what you *think* **could** happen. It isn't real. It is just a story that your mind is making up, and when you believe it, you feed it your energy and give more life to your anxiety.

Consider, what stories does your mind tell you that contribute to your DPDR? How often does your mind worry about the future? Does your mind try to be a fortune-teller? No one knows the future. When you're worried, try to remind yourself that you don't know how things will play out.

Anxiety wants you to worry. It's trying to keep you safe, but it destroys your peace of mind in the process. So, try to remember that although the future is uncertain, things may work out differently than you expected. For this reason, it's important to let go of your expectations about the future and just continue to be present and open.

Returning to the Present

Allowing your thoughts to pull you away from the present moment is like living in your imagination, rather than living in the real world. The first time I really became aware of the present moment, I was stopped at a red light.

Somehow in that moment, everything seemed so vibrant and wonderful. I looked up at the clouds and saw how they moved against the blue sky. Then, I looked around at the other drivers and I could see how wrapped up they were in their minds. No one seemed aware of the present moment. I was very alert, yet relaxed, and I was aware of everything around me.

My mind was quiet, and I began to feel this joy moving in me as I noticed my breathing. Have you noticed how good it feels to just breathe? It is only when you learn to focus on the present moment, that you can be rid of past pain and future uncertainties.

Children and animals are naturally present. Were you more present when you were a child? Personally, I can't say that I was, but if you were, did you experience DPDR back then?

Always remember, the past is gone, and the future is imaginary and full of innumerable possibilities. What is real, is this moment right now in which you read these words. In this moment, everything is okay. All the traumas of the past cease to exist and all the anxieties of the future are washed away in the presence of now.

With mindfulness, you'll re-learn to withdraw your attention from your mind and potentially release unhealed pain from the past that unconsciously resides in you. All the toxic mind-patterns will fall away as you practice returning to the here and now.

5 Minute Mindful Moment Activity

Use this 5-Minute Mindful Activity to:

- Practice returning your attention to the present moment.

- Find your center and rebalance yourself for the day.

- Manage your stress and anxiety.

- Slow down and embrace the present moment.

- Find peace and clarity.

5 Minute Mindful Moment

EASY MINDFULNESS PRACTICE TO REDUCE STRESS

MINDFULNESS SKILLS:
- Observe with curiosity
- Allow things to be, without trying to change them
- Let go of any expectations you have

Become aware of your body, what sensations do you feel? (i.e. warmth, tingingling, tension)   1 MIN

What sounds can you hear? (i.e. computer, distant cars, your breath).   1 MIN

What do you see around you? (i.e. people, places, things, colors).   1 MIN

Close your eyes, relax your body, and take a few conscious breaths.   2 MIN
When you open your eyes write yourself a message for today.
Don't over think it. Write what your heart moves you to write.

5 Minute Mindful Moment

EASY MINDFULNESS PRACTICE TO REDUCE STRESS

MINDFULNESS SKILLS:
- Observe with curiosity
- Allow things to be, without trying to change them
- Let go of any expectations you have

Become aware of your body, what sensations do you feel? (i.e. warmth, tingingling, tension)   1 MIN

What sounds can you hear? (i.e. computer, distant cars, your breath).   1 MIN

What do you see around you? (i.e. people, places, things, colors).   1 MIN

Close your eyes, relax your body, and take a few conscious breaths.   2 MIN
When you open your eyes write yourself a message for today.
Don't over think it. Write what your heart moves you to write.

5 Minute Mindful Moment

EASY MINDFULNESS PRACTICE TO REDUCE STRESS

MINDFULNESS SKILLS:
- Observe with curiosity
- Allow things to be, without trying to change them
- Let go of any expectations you have

Become aware of your body, what sensations do you feel? (i.e. warmth, tingingling, tension)   1 MIN

What sounds can you hear? (i.e. computer, distant cars, your breath).   1 MIN

What do you see around you? (i.e. people, places, things, colors).   1 MIN

Close your eyes, relax your body, and take a few conscious breaths.   2 MIN
When you open your eyes write yourself a message for today.
Don't over think it. Write what your heart moves you to write.

Practice: Mindful Breathing

Every moment our breath is going in and out, yet we rarely slow down to take notice of our breathing.

With conscious breathing, you make the breath the focus of your attention to connect more deeply to the present moment. This shifts your attention from incessant thinking to your inner-being.

Practicing deep breathing and conscious breathing reduces our stress response.

Right now, become aware of your in-breath and out-breath. Spend a few minutes breathing deeply and notice how air moves in through your nostrils and down into the lungs. Then, observe the air as it leaves the body and brushes your upper lip.

Next, take your time and feel your belly rise and fall with each inhale and each exhale.

Let your breathing fall into its natural rhythm without trying to control the breath. Notice how good it feels to just breathe.

After, see if you can become aware of the turning points of your breathing as the breath turns from inhale to exhale.

Spend some time now taking a few conscious breaths. If a thought comes, notice what is on your mind and gently bring your attention back to your breathing.

In the beginning, your mind may wander a lot, but this is normal. It is a sign of progress because it means you are becoming more conscious of the nature of your mind. So, be patient with your practice because it takes time to train the mind.

Start with 5 minutes at a time focusing on your breathing, especially when you feel ungrounded. Once you get used to practicing mindful breathing, you can close your eyes and extend your practice period to 10 minutes or more.

You can practice mindful breathing anywhere and at any time to center yourself.

Section 3: Practice

Debunking the Symptoms

Mindful Sorting Activity

Key Concepts to Transcending Depersonalization

Becoming Conscious of Your Thought Patterns

Observe your Thoughts and Find Clarity

Facing Your Emotions

Connecting with Your Body

Connecting with Your Environment and Senses

Mindful Eating Activity

Daily 5-Step Process for Healing

Defuse Your DPDR Triggers

Debunking the Symptoms

Investigating and Separating the Mental from the Physical and Emotional

When you are clear on the difference between your thoughts, emotions, and physical sensations, you will see how your thinking permeates throughout your experience.

> **Investigate this by asking yourself:**
>
> 1. What am I feeling in my body? What physical sensations are present?
>
> 2. How am I feeling emotionally? What is my mood?

Keep in mind, feeling like you are living in a dream, is neither a physical sensation nor an emotion because physical sensations are tangible. So, "feeling like you are living in a dream", is an *interpretation* of your experience.

Moreover, your physical experience may vary. For example, you may experience pressure around your head, or maybe your eyes are watery, or your eyes are unfocused or crossed. On the other hand, you may not be experiencing any notable sensations at all.

The Symptoms for Depersonalization and Derealization are Mental, Rather than Physical or Emotional, Here's Why:

If you look at the list of DPDR symptoms, you will notice that they are full of **metaphors and similes**. They are more abstract and symbolic, rather than literal. If they were literal, your head *would be wrapped in cotton.* There would literally be a *glass wall in front of you.*

When you examine the list of DPDR symptoms from various sources, they only *point* to the DPDR experience. They say it is "like" living in a dream. And it is "as if" you can't control what you do or say. It is a symbolic description of what we think about our experience. So, what is the reality aside from thinking?

Feeling "empty" or "unreal" or "detached" from your body is just a thought, although this may seem real to you.

You feel this way because your attention is not focused on your body. In fact, it is not possible to be alive without a body. If you think you are detached from your body, then your body will become detached from your awareness.

This is a psychological detachment, not a physical one.

Of course, the thought 'I'm in the body' or 'I'm outside the body' makes no difference to the ability to be aware of your body. Your body is present, and when you focus on it without conceptualization, your experience will feel natural because no thoughts are distracting you from simply being. In fact, awareness of the body is a shared experience that all sentient beings have. How you feel about the body or the way that you experience it, can be influenced by your mind.

When you look in the mirror you *know* that the image is you. Although the longer you stare, the more likely it is that thought will enter your mind. As a result, you are no longer purely *looking* at your reflection. Instead, you are *thinking* about it and *interpreting* it. Eventually, this becomes automatic. And the next time you look in the mirror, the same thoughts about your reflection habitually enter your mind.

Affirming Reality

Try looking in the mirror and saying, "*My name is _____, and I am __ years old. Today is _____. This is me. This is what I look like. This is my body.*" Repeat this 4-6 times without expecting immediate changes. Instead, focus on cultivating self-compassion and affirming this to yourself. And feel free to change the wording to suit you better. You can also extend this to your loved ones, "*This is my partner, this is my child, this is my dad,*" etc. For this part, I prefer to say it in my mind. But when I'm looking in the mirror, I prefer to speak the words out loud. Do what feels right to you. You can also utilize touch by gently touching your face and saying: *this is my face.*

Affirming these truths can help resolve the unconscious DPDR thoughts. And although it may be obvious to some that DPDR symptoms are thought-based, it was not obvious to me. Being unaware of how identified I was with my mind was the source of my pain. Subsequently, once these thoughts are seen as mere thoughts and removed, the effect is complete healing. So, be open to these concepts and to using affirmations regularly because your openness is crucial to healing DPDR.

Here is a poem inspired by DPDR that I wrote in high school.
Can you see the dissociative thought patterns and metaphors (symbolism)?

Empty: (Excerpt) 05/04/2003

Resting,
Decaying,
Drowning in a sea of nothingness,
Breathing in the emptiness.
Filling my lungs with timeless dread.
Drained and forgotten,
Striving to find a purpose,
Inside I feel so dead.
Yet here I move and speak
without meaning.
Lost and weak in a constant void.
The hours awaiting,
No words can define my existence.
So lost for words, so lost.
Lost without a way.
Such life moves around me,
Yet, I alone am left with featherless wings.
Stranded in a desert, trying to move my fins...
I float freely into the emptiness.
And embrace the kingdom of my eternity,
A deep void of nothingness.

DPDR and Metaphors

I once fell from a 12ft height while bouldering (indoor rock climbing), resulting in whiplash and a concussion. Being so disconnected from my body, I didn't realize the severity of my injury. I just knew *I felt off* and that *something didn't feel right*. Metaphors became my way of expressing my needs to my physiotherapist. Hence, feeling like *I was on a train*, meant I was *dizzy*. The mind-body connection gets creative during dissociation. Instead of experiencing sensation, the mind may present imagery and metaphors. So, don't be afraid to express yourself this way. It's a useful tool and a perfectly acceptable means of communication. Ask yourself: *what is this imagery or metaphor trying to communicate? What is it standing in for?*

Now What?

I would not invalidate the lived experience of DPDR, that wouldn't serve anyone. I logically knew I wasn't in an alternate reality, but it didn't change the way I *felt*. My hope is that this book will point you to the cause of your experience and show you how to connect back to your body, other people, your life, and the world around you.

This doesn't mean you need to *reject* DPDR. That's not what making peace is about. Resistance only makes DPDR worse. Furthermore, even if you *understand* how your thoughts are influencing your reality, your experience will only change when those thoughts fall into the background and mindful awareness becomes the foreground.

This healing process is about learning to accept each moment and grow in *self-awareness*. It is about cultivating *self-love* and *self-compassion* and learning to be *aware* of existence beyond the veil of the mind. Mindful awareness alone is healing.

Thoughts are Not Facts

For a long time, my therapist kept telling me, "thoughts are not facts" and although I understood her statement, I didn't grasp what it meant *for me*. It wasn't until I began practicing mindfulness and meditation that I understood her meaning; I didn't realize how seriously I had been taking my mind.

She was right, but I wasn't ready to appreciate her profound statement. It is only now that I understand why she kept repeating it too, whether it was intentional or not.

You see, we fall into negative and unhelpful patterns of thinking through repetition, and through repetition, we can break the cycle.

We are so used to listening to our mind that we don't question it or see its impact. Yet, thoughts have no reality without your belief in them.

All this needs to be experienced, not just intellectually understood. For this reason, the worksheets and practices are such a vital part of this self-help guide and workbook. Some worksheets help you explore your mind, body, and emotions. Others return your attention to the present moment and reconnect you to life. As simple as these practices may seem, please don't discount them. Try to use them regularly because everything that healed me is contained within this book. And I know firsthand that mindfulness dissolves DPDR symptoms and can lead to a full recovery.

Mindful Sorting Activity

Understanding the ideas in this book is a step, but more importantly, building your awareness will help you heal depersonalization and derealization.

Remember, it is important to distinguish your thoughts, emotions, and physical experience. **This activity reveals the patterns that maintain DPDR and helps you become more present.**

Use the *Mindful Sorting Activity* provided on the following page. Practice at least once a week to build your awareness and ground yourself in the present moment.

Each time you complete this activity, objectively look over your worksheet to ensure that everything has been appropriately placed. Take extra care to notice when *thoughts* are appearing as emotions or physical sensations.

Mindful Sorting Activity

FIND CLARITY AND SPACE FROM THOUGHTS, EMOTIONS, AND PHYSICAL SENSATIONS

MINDFULNESS SKILLS:
-Let go of judgment - Allow things to be - Observe with curiosity

INSTRUCTIONS:
- Find a comfortable space where you can sit quietly and will not be disturbed
- Take a moment to center yourself by taking a few deep breaths and relaxing your body
- Tune into your thoughts, emotions, and physical sensations
- Sort your inner-experience into the appropriate section
- Be specific and detailed
- Take your time and notice everything you are experiencing with curiosity
- Accept and allow your experience without trying to change it

THOUGHTS

EMOTIONS

PHYSICAL SENSATIONS

Mindful Sorting Activity

FIND CLARITY AND SPACE FROM THOUGHTS, EMOTIONS, AND PHYSICAL SENSATIONS

MINDFULNESS SKILLS:
-Let go of judgment - Allow things to be - Observe with curiosity

---

INSTRUCTIONS:

- Find a comfortable space where you can sit quietly and will not be disturbed
- Take a moment to center yourself by taking a few deep breaths and relaxing your body
- Tune into your thoughts, emotions, and physical sensations
- Sort your inner-experience into the appropriate section
- Be specific and detailed
- Take your time and notice everything you are experiencing with curiosity
- Accept and allow your experience without trying to change it

THOUGHTS

EMOTIONS

PHYSICAL SENSATIONS

Mindful Sorting Activity

FIND CLARITY AND SPACE FROM THOUGHTS, EMOTIONS, AND PHYSICAL SENSATIONS

MINDFULNESS SKILLS:
-Let go of judgment - Allow things to be - Observe with curiosity

INSTRUCTIONS:

- Find a comfortable space where you can sit quietly and will not be disturbed
- Take a moment to center yourself by taking a few deep breaths and relaxing your body
- Tune into your thoughts, emotions, and physical sensations
- Sort your inner-experience into the appropriate section
- Be specific and detailed
- Take your time and notice everything you are experiencing with curiosity
- Accept and allow your experience without trying to change it

THOUGHTS

EMOTIONS

PHYSICAL SENSATIONS

By practicing the mindful sorting activity, you will be able to separate thought from emotion and physical experiencing, and this will make all the difference.

Continue to practice the Mindful Sorting Activity regularly because it is one of the most important practices in this book for DPDR sufferers.

When you're wrapped up in your mind, the stories your thoughts create pull you in, and appear to affect reality.

Mindful sorting will help you break the cycle of confusing thoughts for emotions and sensations.

You can then look at the three components of your experience and see how your thoughts impact you.

As you do so, your thoughts will not be able to feed your DPDR.

Automatically, dissociation may still occur if there is a trigger, but mindful sorting will also help you to become present when this happens. Then, the dissociation can also dissolve.

Key Concepts to Transcending Depersonalization

#1 Disidentify from your Mind: Mind Spam

Imagine your phone rings and you don't recognize the number, but you answer the call anyway. Immediately you recognize that it's spam and the person on the other end says to you, "you are not real, you have no soul, you are inside a T.V., you are in an alternate reality..."

You can choose to either hang up the phone, entertain the person, or listen to their every word. What happens if you don't hang up?

The thing is, if you don't know it's a spam call, you might fall victim to it. If you know it's spam, you might entertain it but not take it seriously, or you may hang up right away.

It's the same thing we do with our minds. The thoughts we take seriously are the ones we believe. They are the thoughts that pull our attention the most. Sometimes, we entertain thoughts to see where they go and other times, we immediately discard them. For this reason, you don't need to believe everything your mind says. You are free to let go of all the mental commentary.

You have the power to deny your thoughts, but first, you will have to become aware of them hiding in the corners of your psyche.

I remember I used to spend a lot of time researching and reading about my mental health. As a result, I spent a lot of time talking about it, complaining about it, and even writing about it. I spent every moment dwelling on my psychological state, but it only made things worse.

So, I recommend avoiding *unnecessary* research that only feeds into the identity of DPDR. Yes, it is there, you notice it a lot, and it's helpful to learn and talk about DPDR. But you'll know when you're taking things too far because you will feel worse rather than better. Try to notice when you are fixating and ruminating because this will keep you bound. It is best to only talk about DPDR when it serves you.

#2 Facing Your Fear

Be mindful that when you start to shift your awareness away from thinking, you may experience physical sensations and emotions that are unpleasant.

In addition, it may be difficult to withdraw your attention from fear-based thinking. And even harder to face it. It will be scary at first when you start to reconnect with your feelings, your body, your experience, and the world. So, don't push yourself too much or too fast. Just let yourself feel a little at a time. And remember, you are more powerful than your fear.

Note, bringing your attention to these thoughts and sensations does not *create* them. Rather, you are becoming conscious of what has already been there but has been hidden from your awareness.

In fact, there is a lot of fear underneath depersonalization and derealization, and it is the tendency to avoid experiencing fear that perpetuates DPDR.

When you have the courage to face this fear and any pain underlying it, you will break the pattern of dissociation. However, you don't want to go too fast or make yourself feel overwhelmed. The moment you feel overwhelmed, find something enjoyable to do and cultivate self-acceptance and self-compassion. For those with trauma or who need support to work through their inner turmoil, I recommend working with a Somatic Experiencing Therapist.

A good therapist or psychiatrist can help you move through the discomfort of anxious feelings in your body if you are unable to do so on your own.

Remember, the physical experience of fear is uncomfortable, but the fear itself is not dangerous. As you learn to allow yourself to experience fear, it will no longer bother you in the same way. Your desire to heal, will overcome this fear.

#3 Overcome Habitual Existential Thinking

Existential thinking is also quite common among DPDR sufferers, and it can be difficult to let go of.

You may have thoughts like:

- *Why am I here?*
- *What is the purpose of life?*
- *Am I real?*
- *What happens when I die?*
- *Who am I?*

These questions are often repetitive and can go on for years. Perhaps you will find purpose in your life or discover who you are, but consider the following:

- *Will any answer be truly satisfying?*
- *Do these answers even exist?*
- *Are you holding on too tightly to these questions?*
- *What has been the positive impact of entertaining these questions, and what has been the negative impact?*
- *If you did find the answers, would it change anything?*
- *What would it change, aside from now having answers?*
- *Can you accept that there will be things that you do not know?*
- *Can you be okay with not knowing?*
- *How would you feel if you were to let go of all the existential questions and thoughts?*

The reason these questions pull your attention so strongly is due to *fear*. In searching for the answer, you are looking for *peace*. However, it is more important to face the fear than the questions themselves.

The 3 Most Common Existential Thoughts:

Life/Death: What happens when we die?

Acknowledging that life is impermanent means knowing that death is inescapable. Many people are afraid of dying and this fear can prevent you from living. The uncertainty of death causes the mind to ruminate and at times imagine the worst outcomes.

However, making peace with death allows you to live more fully and appreciate life. So, it is important to face the fear of death because the reality of life is that it ends. In other words, face the fear, not the question "what happens when you die" because this question is unanswerable.

Purpose: Why AM I here/What is my purpose?

Life is quite miraculous, and the most amazing function of life is simply being alive! However, everybody wants a grand purpose, yet purpose is the meaning we assign to what we do. This meaning is arbitrary, relative, and self-created.

Consider that your purpose is only whatever you are doing in the present moment. Right now, my purpose is to write this sentence, while yours is to read it. Later, you may go for a walk and in that moment, walking becomes your purpose. You don't need a grand purpose because you are already complete.

The Self: Who Am I?

The function of the mind is to think, you are the one who hears thoughts. So, don't attempt to know yourself through thinking because you have the ability to agree or disagree with thoughts.

If you conceptualize yourself, then you reduce yourself to a mere idea. The concept of yourself is always changing. So, endeavor to find out who you are by *being*, rather than by *thinking*.

In my own experience, constant existential thinking was the last hurdle that I needed to overcome. So, I started to notice every time I had an existential thought. I became aware of the frequency, time, energy, and fascination I had with this type of thinking.

I would become lost in my mind's philosophies, and though I enjoyed it at times, other times it made me feel afraid and confused. I had so much fear in me, and I realized the uncertainties that my existential thinking was obsessing over were due to anxiety. I wanted answers to all the questions to put my mind at ease.

For years, existential thoughts plagued my mind, yet rarely offered any answers. I had to choose freedom because nothing was going to give my mind the answers it wanted. Eventually, I was able to let the thoughts go. They are like spam calls, so, I don't fall for them in the same way. At some point, the negative impact of holding on to existential thinking is more harmful than helpful. This pattern is often unsatisfying and creates suffering within your being.

Furthermore, not every answer is worth conceptualizing. For instance, the experience of love is more profound than the philosophy of it. Additionally, thinking about who you are is not the same as simply being as you are.

Learning to be okay with not knowing is a part of life. Don't cling too tightly to your thoughts, no matter how important they seem. Recognize the impact it has, know when to let go, and let your mind rest in the present moment where you are free.

"Hard it is to train the mind, which goes where it likes and does what it wants. An unruly mind suffers and causes suffering whatever it does. But a well-trained mind brings health and happiness."

— The Dhammapada

Becoming Conscious of Your Thought Patterns

I didn't think I needed to analyze my thoughts because I was already aware that my mind never stopped talking. I would lay in bed at 4AM trying to get my mind to fall into silence, but it wouldn't.

Meditation and mindfulness seemed impossible. But this isn't about "getting rid" of thoughts. Instead, it is about seeing their unreality, their untruths, and their transient nature.

As you go about your day, start listening to your mind. Notice any thoughts that come up. This takes practice because we are not used to actively looking at our own thoughts since they happen automatically and without effort.

The more you look at your thoughts, the more you build awareness and see your mind's tendency to thinking, negativity, and dissatisfaction.

You will also see how quickly your mind jumps from one thing to another. As you begin to pay attention in a new way, you will learn a lot about the nature of your mind.

THOUGHT AWARENESS

As you begin to consciously observe your mind, see which of the following statements are true:

1. Thoughts are powerless without your belief in them.
2. Thoughts dissolve when you withdraw your attention from them.
3. Opposing thoughts can exist in your mind.
4. You have the power to deny your thoughts.
5. Most thoughts aren't important.
6. You are not your thoughts, however, you can be aware of thoughts.
7. You can choose which thoughts to listen to and disregard the rest.
8. Thoughts are repetitive.
9. Thoughts can influence your mood.
10. Thoughts can be negative or positive.
11. Thoughts can be helpful or hurtful.
12. Thoughts can be conscious and unconscious.
13. Thoughts just happen automatically.
14. Your thoughts don't exist without you.
15. Thoughts don't always need to be taken seriously.
16. Thoughts are not always significant.
17. Thoughts are not always true.
18. Not all thoughts pull your attention.
19. Thoughts are not always original.
20. Thoughts are influenced by other people, what you read, what you see, what you hear, and what you've experienced.
21. You are more powerful than your thoughts.
22. You don't need to believe your thoughts.
23. Interpretations are thoughts.
24. Judgments are thoughts.
25. Opinions are also thoughts.
26. Thoughts can be changed.
27. Thoughts can be challenged.
28. The untrained mind has a constant stream of thought.
29. Thoughts can cloud reality and affect how you see things.
30. You can train your mind so will not be a prisoner of thoughts.

Observe Your Thoughts and Find Clarity

To practice observing your thoughts, use the following worksheet to:

- Discover what thoughts currently impact your life now.

- Recognize which thoughts are feeding your DPDR.

- Learn which thoughts grab your attention the most and why.

- Understand your mind's tendencies and what changes you can make.

- Find out what prevents you from having peace and freedom.

Observe Your Thoughts & Find Clarity

LEARN WHAT THOUGHTS CURRENTLY IMPACT YOUR LIFE THE MOST

MINDFULNESS SKILLS:

- Show yourself compassion - Do not judge yourself - Let go of expectations

What thoughts are on your mind right now?

What thoughts grab your attention the most?

Are the thoughts that pull your attention more: Negative ◯ or Positive ◯

Rate how much you believe these thoughts to be true _____
1 - 10

What questions cross your mind the most in your life?

How much time do you spend thinking about these questions? _____

What emotions do you experience when you focus on these thoughts and questions?

How have these thoughts impacted your life?

How would you feel without these thoughts?

How do you currently manage your thoughts and feelings? Is it helpful or hurtful?

How can you challenge these thoughts and change your perspective?

What are you committed to doing to move forward?

Observe Your Thoughts & Find Clarity

LEARN WHAT THOUGHTS CURRENTLY IMPACT YOUR LIFE THE MOST

MINDFULNESS SKILLS:
- Show yourself compassion - Do not judge yourself - Let go of expectations

What thoughts are on your mind right now?

What thoughts grab your attention the most?

Are the thoughts that pull your attention more: Negative ◯   or   Positive ◯

Rate how much you believe these thoughts to be true _____
1 - 10

What questions cross your mind the most in your life?

How much time do you spend thinking about these questions? _____

What emotions do you experience when you focus on these thoughts and questions?

How have these thoughts impacted your life?

How would you feel without these thoughts?

How do you currently manage your thoughts and feelings? Is it helpful or hurtful?

How can you challenge these thoughts and change your perspective?

What are you committed to doing to move forward?

Observe Your Thoughts & Find Clarity

LEARN WHAT THOUGHTS CURRENTLY IMPACT YOUR LIFE THE MOST

MINDFULNESS SKILLS:
- Show yourself compassion - Do not judge yourself - Let go of expectations

What thoughts are on your mind right now?

What thoughts grab your attention the most?

Are the thoughts that pull your attention more: Negative ◯   or   Positive ◯

Rate how much you believe these thoughts to be true _____
1 - 10

What questions cross your mind the most in your life?

How much time do you spend thinking about these questions? _____

What emotions do you experience when you focus on these thoughts and questions?

How have these thoughts impacted your life?

How would you feel without these thoughts?

How do you currently manage your thoughts and feelings? Is it helpful or hurtful?

How can you challenge these thoughts and change your perspective?

What are you committed to doing to move forward?

RETHINK DPDR

DPDR THOUGHT	RETHINK DPDR
I feel weird/strange	My mind is interpreting my experience as weird/strange
I don't recognize myself in the mirror	I know that this image is me
I don't feel anything	I can feel my body and the surface that it is on.
I feel like I am living in a dream, everything looks pixelated	I know I am awake, and I know that this is reality
I feel empty	Empty is not a feeling
This doesn't seem real	I know that this is real
My loved one seems like a stranger	My loved one is not a stranger, but my thoughts about them are making them seem strange to me
My body is moving automatically, I feel like a robot.	Both conscious and subconscious movements happen in the body. I can choose my movements.
I don't understand the nature of my reality	Living in the mind is *not reality*. Reality can only be experienced, not conceptualized

No matter how unique, philosophical, important, or true a DPDR thought seems, **you can find a way to rethink it.** If you need help rethinking your DPDR thoughts, ask someone you trust. This process isn't something you need to do alone. So, reach out when needed and be honest with yourself about which thoughts you give your energy to.

Facing Your Emotions

Healing depersonalization may require you to face unpleasant emotions. Remember, the goal is to reconnect to your experience, even when there is discomfort.

Don't forget, fear has been the root cause of your dissociation. To move beyond this, you must learn to allow emotions to have their place in your life.

If emotions are rejected and resisted, your suffering will persist. So, remember this anytime you are faced with painful emotions.

In the beginning, it may take extra effort to identify your feelings and you may not be familiar with your experience due to DPDR, so be patient with this process.

Once you learn how to tune into your emotional state and face what you are feeling, it will be easier to weather the storms within.

"This too shall pass."

Process Your Emotions

Let's try to connect with and process your emotions as they relate to your DPDR.

The next time you experience DPDR, or if you are experiencing your symptoms now, use this worksheet to:

- Become aware of how thoughts affect your experience.

- Work through any difficult emotions.

- Understand your feelings and make peace with them.

- Process how you feel in a healthy way.

- Avoid getting swept away by your feelings.

- Build self-compassion.

- Receive insights and access your inner guidance.

Process your Emotions

OBSERVE, UNDERSTAND, AND MAKE PEACE WITH HOW YOU FEEL

MINDFULNESS SKILLS:
- Show yourself compassion - Do not judge yourself - Let go of expectations

How are you feeling? Name your emotions.

INTENSITY

1 - 10   1 - 10   1 - 10

Where in your body do you experience these emotions?

How much do you want these feelings to go away? _____
1 - 10

What event prompted this emotion? (who, what, where, and when)

What are your thoughts, beliefs, assumptions & interpretations about the situation?

What is your body language right now?

What do you feel like saying/doing?

What would accepting this emotion look and feel like?

What advice would you give someone you love in this situation?

How can you show yourself love and compassion while you experience this emotion?

Process your Emotions

OBSERVE, UNDERSTAND, AND MAKE PEACE WITH HOW YOU FEEL

MINDFULNESS SKILLS:
- Show yourself compassion - Do not judge yourself - Let go of expectations

How are you feeling? Name your emotions.

INTENSITY

1 - 10   1 - 10   1 - 10

Where in your body do you experience these emotions?

How much do you want these feelings to go away? _____
1 - 10

What event prompted this emotion? (who, what, where, and when)

What are your thoughts, beliefs, assumptions & interpretations about the situation?

What is your body language right now?

What do you feel like saying/doing?

What would accepting this emotion look and feel like?

What advice would you give someone you love in this situation?

How can you show yourself love and compassion while you experience this emotion?

Process your Emotions

OBSERVE, UNDERSTAND, AND MAKE PEACE WITH HOW YOU FEEL

MINDFULNESS SKILLS:
- Show yourself compassion - Do not judge yourself - Let go of expectations

How are you feeling? Name your emotions.

INTENSITY

1 - 10   1 - 10   1 - 10

Where in your body do you experience these emotions?

How much do you want these feelings to go away? _____
1 - 10

What event prompted this emotion? (who, what, where, and when)

What are your thoughts, beliefs, assumptions & interpretations about the situation?

What is your body language right now?

What do you feel like saying/doing?

What would accepting this emotion look and feel like?

What advice would you give someone you love in this situation?

How can you show yourself love and compassion while you experience this emotion?

Connecting with Your Body

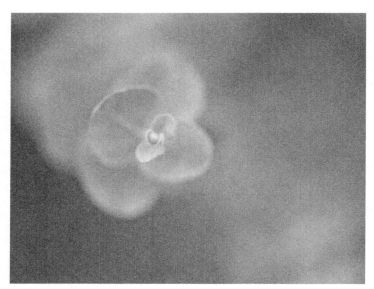

The first time I did a body awareness meditation was in group therapy. I was late and my social anxiety was freaking out. My heart was pounding so hard. I was ashamed of myself for walking into the class late.

I had overslept, woke up in a hurry, didn't eat, and when I walked into the room, I wanted to cry. Yet, no one seemed to notice how frazzled I was.

We were about to start a guided body meditation, and I was relieved when they turned off the lights and told us all to lie down and close our eyes. *Thank God*, I thought, not wanting anyone to look at me in case I cried. As we began meditating, I became aware of all the fear I felt.

It seemed to be predominantly in my stomach, but 10 minutes into the meditation, when I observed my body with mindful awareness, the fear had dissolved. I couldn't find it anymore, it wasn't anywhere!

Instead, I noticed my belly rising and falling with the breath and I felt perfectly at peace. Our body is the vehicle that carries us through life, it is alive and when you become still, you discover a peaceful energy moving through it.

The body is a wonderful focus for practicing mindfulness. Remember, the pattern of DPDR is to disconnect from the body, so, building awareness of the body is imperative.

Body Awareness

To build awareness of your body, use the following worksheet to:

- Become aware of your bodily sensations.

- Reconnect with your body on a deeper level.

- Find calm and relaxation.

- Reduce tension and anxiety.

- Center yourself in the present moment.

Body Awareness

FIND CALM AND RELAXATION THROUGH CONNECTING TO YOUR BODY

INSTRUCTIONS: Scan the area of your body outlined below and notice what sensations, if any, are present. Write your observations in the spaces provided. Examples of sensations: warmth, cold, tingling, pressure, tightness, aching, throbbing, numbness, etc.

Feet

Front and back of calves

Thighs

Hips

Back

Stomach

Chest

Arms

Face and Head

Whole body

Body Awareness

FIND CALM AND RELAXATION THROUGH CONNECTING TO YOUR BODY

INSTRUCTIONS: Scan the area of your body outlined below and notice what sensations, if any, are present. Write your observations in the spaces provided. Examples of sensations: warmth, cold, tingling, pressure, tightness, aching, throbbing, numbness, etc.

Feet

Front and back of calves

Thighs

Hips

Back

Stomach

Chest

Arms

Face and Head

Whole body

Body Awareness

FIND CALM AND RELAXATION THROUGH CONNECTING TO YOUR BODY

INSTRUCTIONS: Scan the area of your body outlined below and notice what sensations, if any, are present. Write your observations in the spaces provided. Examples of sensations: warmth, cold, tingling, pressure, tightness, aching, throbbing, numbness, etc.

_____

Feet

Front and back of calves

Thighs

Hips

Back

Stomach

Chest

Arms

Face and Head

Whole body

Connecting with Your Environment and Senses

Right now, look around and try not to label, analyze, or interpret what you see. Notice if your mind steps in to make assessments about what you perceive.

See everything as if you're seeing it for the first time. Pretend you don't know what anything is or what it's for. Just observe.

In this moment, just be conscious of your surroundings, is there something that you are aware of now that you didn't notice before?

Touch the fabric of your clothing, you don't need to interpret it as soft or rough, just feel it. If you have some water near you, take a sip, and really taste it. Again, don't interpret or judge.

Close your eyes for a moment, notice any sounds, what do you hear? Stretch your hearing as far as you can, and just be aware of all that you can hear.

What enters your field of perception?

No matter where you are, being conscious of your sense perceptions anchors you in the present moment. When eating, taste your food. Really notice the flavors.

If you have flowers in your home or garden, smell them! Observe your sense of touch when doing the dishes or washing your face.

I really hope you'll love the next mindful practice as much as I do. It's one of my favorite ones: *Mindful Eating.*

The first time, I used a nectarine for my practice, and the experience was so delightful and memorable. The second time was truly eye-opening.

It was in one of my therapy groups, and for some reason they chose raisins. I thought, *ewww! I **hate** raisins! Who chose raisins?*

I really thought I hated raisins. Turns out, during the exercise I enjoyed them and found them rather sweet.

This is how powerful non-judging in mindfulness is. Our minds can have us convinced we don't like something that we do like.

So, for this exercise, do it a few times on different days, trying different foods. Try something you like, something you don't like, and if possible, something you don't eat very often or have not tried before.

Mindful Eating

To develop mindfulness of your senses, use the mindful eating worksheet to:

- Reconnect to your body and senses.

- Experience food in a new and profound way.

- Enjoy the experience of eating.

- Practice non-judging.

- Slow down and relish in the present moment.

- Expand your awareness.

Mindful Eating

ENJOY THE EXPERIENCE OF EATING AND SLOWING DOWN

INSTRUCTIONS:
- Choose food that you can eat by hand (i.e. apple, peach, cookie, sandwich)
- Get rid of all distractions. Sit somewhere you can practice eating in full awareness
- Really take your time with this exercise and relish in each moment. Don't rush.

Before you begin eating, consider the origins of your food. What was its journey to get to you? Where did it come from? What went in to preparing it? Be detailed & specific. Spend a few moments in contemplation and write your findings. `2 MIN`

Hold the food in your hands and close your eyes for a moment. Use your finger tips and notice what you feel. Describe the feeling and texture as much as you can. `2 MIN`

Bring the food to your nose, close your eyes, & notice its fragrance. Does it smell the same on all sides? Does it smell sweet? Breathe deeply and really notice the odour. `2 MIN`

Now, look at your food as if you are looking at it for the first time. What do you see? What colors are there? What shapes and shades are there? Again, be descriptive. `2 MIN`

Bring the food towards your mouth and pause before taking a bite. What sensations do you notice in your mouth as it prepares for the food? `2 MIN`

Slowly take a bite of your food but don't swallow it yet. Relish in tasting it. Take note of the texture, the taste, is it dry or juicy? Notice your reflex to swallow and as you do be aware of how it feels as the food slides into your system. What do you notice? `2 MIN`

What are your takeaways from this practice?

Mindful Eating

ENJOY THE EXPERIENCE OF EATING AND SLOWING DOWN

INSTRUCTIONS:
- Choose food that you can eat by hand (i.e. apple, peach, cookie, sandwich)
- Get rid of all distractions. Sit somewhere you can practice eating in full awareness
- Really take your time with this exercise and relish in each moment. Don't rush.

Before you begin eating, consider the origins of your food. What was its journey to   2 MIN
get to you? Where did it come from? What went in to preparing it? Be detailed &
specific. Spend a few moments in contemplation and write your findings.

Hold the food in your hands and close your eyes for a moment. Use your finger tips   2 MIN
and notice what you feel. Describe the feeling and texture as much as you can.

Bring the food to your nose, close your eyes, & notice its fragrance. Does it smell the   2 MIN
same on all sides? Does it smell sweet? Breathe deeply and really notice the odour.

Now, look at your food as if you are looking at it for the first time. What do you see?   2 MIN
What colors are there? What shapes and shades are there? Again, be descriptive.

Bring the food towards your mouth and pause before taking a bite. What sensations 2 MIN
do you notice in your mouth as it prepares for the food?

Slowly take a bite of your food but don't swallow it yet. Relish in tasting it. Take note   2 MIN
of the texture, the taste, is it dry or juicy? Notice your reflex to swallow and as you do
be aware of how it feels as the food slides into your system. What do you notice?

What are your takeaways from this practice?

Mindful Eating

ENJOY THE EXPERIENCE OF EATING AND SLOWING DOWN

INSTRUCTIONS:
- Choose food that you can eat by hand (i.e. apple, peach, cookie, sandwich)
- Get rid of all distractions. Sit somewhere you can practice eating in full awareness
- Really take your time with this exercise and relish in each moment. Don't rush.

Before you begin eating, consider the origins of your food. What was its journey to   2 MIN
get to you? Where did it come from? What went in to preparing it? Be detailed &
specific. Spend a few moments in contemplation and write your findings.

Hold the food in your hands and close your eyes for a moment. Use your finger tips   2 MIN
and notice what you feel. Describe the feeling and texture as much as you can.

Bring the food to your nose, close your eyes, & notice its fragrance. Does it smell the   2 MIN
same on all sides? Does it smell sweet? Breathe deeply and really notice the odour.

Now, look at your food as if you are looking at it for the first time. What do you see?   2 MIN
What colors are there? What shapes and shades are there? Again, be descriptive.

Bring the food towards your mouth and pause before taking a bite. What sensations   2 MIN
do you notice in your mouth as it prepares for the food?

Slowly take a bite of your food but don't swallow it yet. Relish in tasting it. Take note   2 MIN
of the texture, the taste, is it dry or juicy? Notice your reflex to swallow and as you do
be aware of how it feels as the food slides into your system. What do you notice?

What are your takeaways from this practice?

Daily 5-Step Process for Healing Depersonalization and Derealization

Growing in Awareness and Discernment

I remember one of the first times I caught my mind in a DPDR pattern. I was looking in the mirror, "feeling" estranged from my image when I heard my mind say "this feels weird... I look strange... this doesn't feel right. I feel like I am inside the mirror.".

Immediately, I shifted my attention to my body and my heart rate was accelerated, my eyes were unfocused, and I was tense. I grounded myself with my breathing and challenged the DPDR thoughts I was having.

I reframed my thoughts, "I know the image is me. I don't feel strange, I feel anxious." I also disengaged from the desire to entertain existential thoughts. I heard my mind in the background wanting to say, "I feel like I'm in an alternate reality".

It may sound silly to those who have not experienced DPDR, but I want to be honest about what thoughts I was entertaining. When I became fully present, these thoughts disappeared, and it was just me looking in the mirror.

When I first started using mindfulness to address my DPDR, I caught so many thoughts about reality. I'd notice how unfocused my eyes were because I was tired and daydreaming, and I was finally able to connect to the fear that lived in my body.

When you experience DPDR, you are going beyond the fear. So, returning to the fear brings you back to the present. When you allow yourself to experience the sensations that fear brings, it may be uncomfortable for a while, but it won't hurt you. In fact, it will allow you to become more connected, and eventually, that fear will also dissolve when you see it is just your mind telling you stories about reality that aren't true.

I've broken down this process for healing into 5-steps that you can use daily when you are faced with symptoms. It will help you notice the triggering thoughts, feel your emotions, and reconnect to life with mindfulness.

Daily 5-Step Process for Healing DPDR

 Become aware of your thoughts.

Separate your thoughts from your emotions, sense perceptions, and physical sensations.

Ask yourself:
- Is my experience a thought? What thoughts do I have?
- Is this experience a mood? How am I feeling?
- What do I physically feel? What sensations are in my body?

Once you identify mind patterns that feed into your DP and DR, acknowledge these thoughts, and let them go.

Say to yourself:
"This is just a thought."

 Ground yourself with mindful breathing and connect back to your body, emotions, environment, and physical sensation through mindful awareness.

DP/DR Trigger Checklist

Can you identify any of the following:

- HAVING EXISTENTIAL OR PHILOSOPHICAL THOUGHTS

- FATIGUE, TIRENESS, OR UNFOCUSED EYES

- FEAR/ANXIETY

- NOT FOCUSED ON THE PRESENT MOMENT

- AVOIDING UNPLEASANT EMOTIONS OR EXPERIENCES

- INTERPRETING YOUR EXPERIENCE

- WITHDRAWING YOUR ATTENTION FROM YOUR BODY OR SURROUNDINGS

- ATTENTION IS CARRIED AWAY BY THOUGHTS

- FEARING YOUR DP/DR AND FORGETTING ITS POSITIVE INTENTION

- OTHER _____

KNOW WHAT'S TRIGGERING YOUR SYMPTOMS SO YOU CAN INTERVENE

Defuse Your DPDR Triggers

BALANCE YOUR MIND, IDENTIFY & CHANGE UNHELPFUL THOUGHT PATTERNS

1. Trigger	2. Reactions	3. Thoughts
What happened? Describe the situation: who, what, where, & when Stick to the facts only. Don't interpret.	What did you do? How did you act/behave? How did you feel (emotions & physical sensations)	What did the experience mean to you? How did you interpret this experience?

4. Proof	5. Helpful/Hurtful	6. Alternate Views
What evidence proves your thoughts are true? What is the evidence against these thoughts?	What are the pros/cons of keeping these thoughts? How are these thought patterns helpful/hurtful?	What are other ways can you look at this? What is more realistic, balanced, compassionate, loving, & helpful?

Defuse Your DPDR Triggers

BALANCE YOUR MIND, IDENTIFY & CHANGE UNHELPFUL THOUGHT PATTERNS

1. Trigger	2. Reactions	3. Thoughts
What happened? Describe the situation: who, what, where, & when Stick to the facts only. Don't interpret.	What did you do? How did you act/behave? How did you feel (emotions & physical sensations)	What did the experience mean to you? How did you interpret this experience?

4. Proof	5. Helpful/Hurtful	6. Alternate Views
What evidence proves your thoughts are true? What is the evidence against these thoughts?	What are the pros/cons of keeping these thoughts? How are these thought patterns helpful/hurtful?	What are other ways can you look at this? What is more realistic, balanced, compassionate, loving, & helpful?

Defuse Your DPDR Triggers

BALANCE YOUR MIND, IDENTIFY & CHANGE UNHELPFUL THOUGHT PATTERNS

1. Trigger	2. Reactions	3. Thoughts
What happened? Describe the situation: who, what, where, & when Stick to the facts only. Don't interpret.	What did you do? How did you act/behave? How did you feel (emotions & physical sensations)	What did the experience mean to you? How did you interpret this experience?
4. Proof	**5. Helpful/Hurtful**	**6. Alternate Views**
What evidence proves your thoughts are true? What is the evidence against these thoughts?	What are the pros/cons of keeping these thoughts? How are these thought patterns helpful/hurtful?	What are other ways can you look at this? What is more realistic, balanced, compassionate, loving, & helpful?

Conclusion

We have discussed the impact of stress, fear, and anxiety when it comes to DPDR. We have also looked at the positive intention of DPDR and how our minds are conditioned to protect us, even if that means detaching from painful experiences.

Additionally, we began building our awareness of our thoughts and seeing how they feed the patterns associated with DPDR.

Some of these patterns include *existential thinking, negative self-talk, identifying with DPDR and the mind, confusing thoughts for physical and emotional sensations, interpreting our experience rather than connecting to it, avoiding painful feelings, resisting our experience, and clinging to hopelessness to name a few.*

These are all things I did when I was struggling with DPDR. I literally believed that I was in an alternate reality. That is how painful DPDR was for me. I couldn't believe that my experience was real. Perhaps you have discovered additional tendencies that feed your DPDR.

Again, we all experience things differently. Whatever your unique experience is, don't judge yourself for your suffering, and know that there is more to you than DPDR.

We have also learned to differentiate our thoughts, emotions, and physical sensations, and to show ourselves kindness and compassion, face our emotions, feel our body, become aware of our senses, and to recognize that we don't need to believe the thoughts associated with DPDR.

Remember, with DPDR our thoughts are at the foreground and everything else is in the background. The mindfulness practices here will help declutter your mind, calm your emotions, and bring you peace. They will help you find your center and reconnect to yourself, your loved ones, and the world around you. So, establishing a mindfulness routine will help you on your healing journey.

THINGS TO REMEMBER

Learning to mindfully redirect your attention to your breathing, body, and sense perceptions will help ground you.

Don't interpret your experience through thought. Instead, simply identify your emotions and physical experience.

If you've had DP/DR for a long time, it may take time to heal. Let go of any expectations you have and accept things as they are now.

As I began to reconnect, I didn't understand my experience. I noticed bodily tension, and had emotions I could not identify. This is a part of the process.

Be patient with yourself and don't judge yourself or your experiences. Instead, show yourself the love and compassion that you need to heal.

Trust that there is a strength within you that hasn't given up for a reason. Know that it is okay to believe in your own freedom.

Establishing an Ongoing Mindfulness Routine

In addition to the Daily 5-Step Process for Healing Depersonalization and Derealization, here's how to create a mindfulness routine for the week, using the worksheets and practices provided in this book.

Consider the following:

What has been your favorite mindfulness exercise from this book? Which practices suit your temperament the most? And which ones do you want to integrate into your life?

Here is an example of a: "Days of the Week" Mindfulness Routine

Monday: 5 Minute Mindfulness Moment Activity
Tuesday: Mindful Sorting Activity
Wednesday: Observe Your Thoughts and Find Clarity Worksheet
Thursday: Process Your Emotions Worksheet
Friday: Connecting with the Body
Saturday: Mindful Eating Activity
Sunday: Reflection

Create your own mindfulness routine based on what works best for you. Remember, mindful breathing can be used at any time and is always accessible to you.

Eventually, you may not need the worksheets for your practice period, and you may want to explore more ways on your own to practice mindfulness in your daily life.

There are additional mindfulness practices and meditations available for free on my website that you can try: inherentpeace.com/free-resources

My Days of the Week Mindfulness Routine

Establish your commitment to the practice part of this book. Fill in your mindfulness routine for the week. Feel free to repeat activities you enjoy!

Options to consider:

- 5 Minute Mindfulness Moment
- Mindful Sorting Activity
- Observe Your Thoughts
- Process Your Emotions
- Connecting with the Body
- Mindful Eating Activity
- Reflection

THURSDAY

MONDAY

FRIDAY

TUESDAY

SATURDAY

WEDNESDAY

SUNDAY

There are more ways to practice mindfulness, visit inherentpeace.com for more

My Life Now

Maybe it's just me, but for years, whenever I tried to talk about DPDR with some mental health professionals, it seemed like their first rule about DPDR was: *we don't talk about DPDR.* Nor do many seem willing to talk about trauma.

What we did talk about was depression, anxiety, sleep disorder, and ADHD. All of which have been calmed and brought into balance through meditation and mindfulness.

Ultimately, it is up to you to do the work to heal. To really grasp the heart of this book, the ideas need to be **practiced**.

For the last seven years, I have dedicated myself to improving my mental health and finding peace. I've spent countless hours researching *ways to heal*, reading, practicing what I was learning, going to therapy, and listening to spiritual teachers. Yet, none of it would have meant anything *if I didn't do my part.*

I had to learn how to face my pain and sit with my fears, anxieties, and sadness. I had to consciously connect to the experiences that DPDR wanted me to avoid. **I felt like I was learning everything for the first time.** It wasn't easy but I was highly motivated because I had reached a point where I didn't want to live anymore. Nothing felt more painful than life. So, I shifted all my efforts toward healing.

When I wake up now, there is no trace of DPDR. If I feel anxious, I focus on body awareness. Whenever I am not peaceful, I observe my thoughts, I challenge them, and I let them go when I must. And if I dissociate, I practice body awareness. But the thoughts that used to turn dissociation into DPDR, no longer pull me in. I see their unreality and they have no effect on me.

It doesn't take time to let go, but it does take time to learn how and when to stop holding on.

Now, I practice mindfulness, meditation, and yoga every day because it enriches my life. It brings me peace, helps me focus, and anchors me through difficult times.

In time, these practices can become an effortless part of your day if you let them, and they will bring you healing.

Full Healing and Freedom from Depersonalization and Derealization

Whatever happens now, accept it, and allow it to be. Continue to make peace with your experience and accept yourself as you are. But know that you are not DPDR, it is just something you experience, and you are stronger than you can ever know.

Whether your DPDR comes or goes, be at peace.

In time, emotions and physical feelings will not create the same suffering as they do now, and your wisdom and understanding will grow.

Moreover, continue to be open to healing, but also do not be attached to the idea that you *need* to heal.

You are perfect as you are and do not need anything more to be complete. Find this self-acceptance inside yourself. Then, you will be free to give yourself the permission to have hope while always accepting whatever the present moment brings.

This gentle acceptance is how you heal your mind and invite peace, not war, into your life and your inner world.

With mindfulness, your symptoms will not only reduce but from my experience, they can disappear completely.

Your fears and pain will also lessen, you will feel more connected, and you will know that you are safe, even when you experience discomfort.

By withdrawing your attention from your mind, you will experience life in a different way; through *being*, not *thinking*.

Your life will become more beautiful, and everything will look and feel more vibrant. You will begin *living* instead of constantly *thinking*.

It will feel like you have finally "returned home," and this is liberating.

May you be free and at peace,

Ravelle

inherentpeace.com

About the Author

Ravelle grew up in Trinidad and Tobago and currently resides in Toronto, Canada. She grew up in a Hindu and Catholic home and has been passionate about spirituality since childhood.

Her lived experience with trauma urged her on a journey of self-discovery. After years of immense psychological suffering, she uncovered a deep peace within her.

Through meditation and self-inquiry, waves of insight, love, and bliss began to flow through her. From these experiences, she realized that she is not her emotional, mental, or physical states, and that the only way to peace and freedom is to turn inward.

Ravelle has been influenced by several spiritual books like the Upanishads, Bhagavad Gita, and Dhammapada. She practices meditation, yoga, mindfulness, and self-inquiry daily.

She is also passionate about sharing the teachings and practices that have inspired her, especially Advaita Vedanta and Eastern philosophy.

Over the years, Ravelle has been sharing spiritual knowledge and working with individuals who want to integrate spirituality into their lives.

She spends as much time as she can in her spiritual practice and hiking in nature, and she enjoys photography, writing, and reading. *Unreality Check: The Mindful Way to Heal Depersonalization and Derealization* is her first self-published book.

You can link up with Ravelle here:

Website: inherentpeace.com
Instagram: @inherentpeace
Pinterest: @inherentpeace

Appendix

- A Letter to DPDR

- 5 Minute Mindful Moment

- Mindful Breathing

- Mindful Sorting Activity

- Observe Your Thoughts and Find Clarity

- Process Your Emotions

- Body Awareness

- Mindful Eating

- My Days of the Week Mindfulness Routine

- Defuse Your DPDR Triggers

A Letter to DP/DR

ACKNOWLEDGE, REFLECT, ACCEPT, AND RELEASE

MINDFULNESS SKILLS:

- Face your pain with openness, compassion, and let go of judgment
- Accept and allow space for your experience to be what it is in this moment

―――――――――――――――

Acknowledge the suffering depersonalization and derealization has caused you. Write as if you are speaking to your DP/DR, tell it how it has affected you, and openly express any pain it has caused you throughout your life.

Reflect on your DP/DR's positive intention and write to it, letting it know you understand the reason it came into your life. If you feel up to it, you can even thank it for being there when you needed it.

Create a short message to yourself for the next time you experience your symptoms to help you make peace with how you are feeling. For example: *I am experiencing DP/DR, and I am going to be okay, it is not here to hurt me, I will allow space for my healing.*

Write to your DP/DR to let it know that it is no longer useful and that you are ready to experience life without it. Let it know what it would mean to you to be free of it.

5 Minute Mindful Moment

EASY MINDFULNESS PRACTICE TO REDUCE STRESS

MINDFULNESS SKILLS:
- Observe with curiosity
- Allow things to be, without trying to change them
- Let go of any expectations you have

Become aware of your body, what sensations do you feel? (i.e. warmth, tingingling, tension)   1 MIN

What sounds can you hear? (i.e. computer, distant cars, your breath).   1 MIN

What do you see around you? (i.e. people, places, things, colors).   1 MIN

Close your eyes, relax your body, and take a few conscious breaths.   2 MIN
When you open your eyes write yourself a message for today.
Don't over think it. Write what your heart moves you to write.

Practice: Mindful Breathing

Every moment our breath is going in and out, yet we rarely slow down to take notice of our breathing.

With conscious breathing, you make the breath the focus of your attention to connect more deeply to the present moment. This shifts your attention from incessant thinking to your inner-being.

Practicing deep breathing and conscious breathing reduces our stress response.

Right now, become aware of your in-breath and out-breath. Spend a few minutes breathing deeply and notice how air moves in through your nostrils and down into the lungs. Then, observe the air as it leaves the body and brushes your upper lip.

Next, take your time and feel your belly rise and fall with each inhale and each exhale.

Let your breathing fall into its natural rhythm without trying to control the breath. Notice how good it feels to just breathe.

After, see if you can become aware of the turning points of your breathing as the breath turns from inhale to exhale.

Spend some time now taking a few conscious breaths. If a thought comes, notice what is on your mind and gently bring your attention back to your breathing.

In the beginning, your mind may wander a lot, but this is normal. It is a sign of progress because it means you are becoming more conscious of the nature of your mind. So, be patient with your practice because it takes time to train the mind.

Start with 5 minutes at a time focusing on your breathing, especially when you feel ungrounded. Once you get used to practicing mindful breathing, you can close your eyes and extend your practice period to 10 minutes or more.

You can practice mindful breathing anywhere and at any time to center yourself.

Mindful Sorting Activity

FIND CLARITY AND SPACE FROM THOUGHTS, EMOTIONS, AND PHYSICAL SENSATIONS

MINDFULNESS SKILLS:
-Let go of judgment - Allow things to be - Observe with curiosity

INSTRUCTIONS:
- Find a comfortable space where you can sit quietly and will not be disturbed
- Take a moment to center yourself by taking a few deep breaths and relaxing your body
- Tune into your thoughts, emotions, and physical sensations
- Sort your inner-experience into the appropriate section
- Be specific and detailed
- Take your time and notice everything you are experiencing with curiosity
- Accept and allow your experience without trying to change it

THOUGHTS

EMOTIONS

PHYSICAL SENSATIONS

Observe Your Thoughts & Find Clarity

LEARN WHAT THOUGHTS CURRENTLY IMPACT YOUR LIFE THE MOST

MINDFULNESS SKILLS:
- Show yourself compassion - Do not judge yourself - Let go of expectations
_____

What thoughts are on your mind right now?

What thoughts grab your attention the most?

Are the thoughts that pull your attention more: Negative ◯   or   Positive ◯

Rate how much you believe these thoughts to be true _____
1 - 10

What questions cross your mind the most in your life?

How much time do you spend thinking about these questions? _____

What emotions do you experience when you focus on these thoughts and questions?

How have these thoughts impacted your life?

How would you feel without these thoughts?

How do you currently manage your thoughts and feelings? Is it helpful or hurtful?

How can you challenge these thoughts and change your perspective?

What are you committed to doing to move forward?

CREATED WITH LOVE BY: RAVELLE - INHERENTPEACE.COM

Process your Emotions

OBSERVE, UNDERSTAND, AND MAKE PEACE WITH HOW YOU FEEL

MINDFULNESS SKILLS:
- Show yourself compassion - Do not judge yourself - Let go of expectations

_____

How are you feeling? Name your emotions.

INTENSITY

1 - 10   1 - 10   1 - 10

Where in your body do you experience these emotions?

How much do you want these feelings to go away? _____
1 - 10

What event prompted this emotion? (who, what, where, and when)

What are your thoughts, beliefs, assumptions & interpretations about the situation?

What is your body language right now?

What do you feel like saying/doing?

What would accepting this emotion look and feel like?

What advice would you give someone you love in this situation?

How can you show yourself love and compassion while you experience this emotion?

Body Awareness

FIND CALM AND RELAXATION THROUGH CONNECTING TO YOUR BODY

INSTRUCTIONS: Scan the area of your body outlined below and notice what sensations, if any, are present. Write your observations in the spaces provided. Examples of sensations: warmth, cold, tingling, pressure, tightness, aching, throbbing, numbness, etc.

Feet

Front and back of calves

Thighs

Hips

Back

Stomach

Chest

Arms

Face and Head

Whole body

CREATED WITH LOVE BY: RAVELLE - INHERENTPEACE.COM

Mindful Eating

ENJOY THE EXPERIENCE OF EATING AND SLOWING DOWN

INSTRUCTIONS:
- Choose food that you can eat by hand (i.e. apple, peach, cookie, sandwich)
- Get rid of all distractions. Sit somewhere you can practice eating in full awareness
- Really take your time with this exercise and relish in each moment. Don't rush.

Before you begin eating, consider the origins of your food. What was its journey to   2 MIN
get to you? Where did it come from? What went in to preparing it? Be detailed &
specific. Spend a few moments in contemplation and write your findings.

Hold the food in your hands and close your eyes for a moment. Use your finger tips   2 MIN
and notice what you feel. Describe the feeling and texture as much as you can.

Bring the food to your nose, close your eyes, & notice its fragrance. Does it smell the   2 MIN
same on all sides? Does it smell sweet? Breathe deeply and really notice the odour.

Now, look at your food as if you are looking at it for the first time. What do you see?   2 MIN
What colors are there? What shapes and shades are there? Again, be descriptive.

Bring the food towards your mouth and pause before taking a bite. What sensations   2 MIN
do you notice in your mouth as it prepares for the food?

Slowly take a bite of your food but don't swallow it yet. Relish in tasting it. Take note   2 MIN
of the texture, the taste, is it dry or juicy? Notice your reflex to swallow and as you do
be aware of how it feels as the food slides into your system. What do you notice?

What are your takeaways from this practice?

My Days of the Week Mindfulness Routine

Establish your commitment to the practice part of this book. Fill in your mindfulness routine for the week. Feel free to repeat activities you enjoy!

Options to consider:

- 5 Minute Mindfulness Moment
- Mindful Sorting Activity
- Observe Your Thoughts
- Process Your Emotions
- Connecting with the Body
- Mindful Eating Activity
- Reflection

THURSDAY

MONDAY

FRIDAY

TUESDAY

SATURDAY

WEDNESDAY

SUNDAY

There are more ways to practice mindfulness, visit inherentpeace.com for more

Defuse Your DPDR Triggers

BALANCE YOUR MIND, IDENTIFY & CHANGE UNHELPFUL THOUGHT PATTERNS

1. Trigger	2. Reactions	3. Thoughts
What happened? Describe the situation: who, what, where, & when Stick to the facts only. Don't interpret.	What did you do? How did you act/behave? How did you feel (emotions & physical sensations)	What did the experience mean to you? How did you interpret this experience?

4. Proof	5. Helpful/Hurtful	6. Alternate Views
What evidence proves your thoughts are true? What is the evidence against these thoughts?	What are the pros/cons of keeping these thoughts? How are these thought patterns helpful/hurtful?	What are other ways can you look at this? What is more realistic, balanced, compassionate, loving, & helpful?

Printed in Great Britain
by Amazon

43617138R00059